Soul*SIMPLIFY*winning

DISCOVER THE *EASE* OF EVANGELISM

Cara A. Salley

A catalogue record for this book is available from the British Library.

Published in the United Kingdom by Salley Publishing.

ISBN: 978-0-9934512-0-1

Design/Layout: Loulita Gill Design

Editors: Terri Pease, Amy White

important

Acknowledgements

Thanks to God for His grace to write this book.

Thanks to my amazing boys who have
encouraged me to finish it.

Thanks to the treasured souls that I've been
privileged to lead to Him and have
brought *life* to this book!

The | # Contents

"You have nothing to do but to save souls."[1]

- John Wesley

---

1   Telford, John. "Wesley Center Online." *The Life of John Wesley*. N.p., n.d. Web.
23 June 2015.

Simplify

Simplify = sim·pli·fy

transitive verb \ *'sim-plə-fī* \

   : to make (something) easier to do or understand

   sim·pli·fied sim·pli·fy·ing

Full Definition of SIMPLIFY

   : to make <u>simple</u> or <u>simpler</u>: as

   a : to reduce to basic essentials

   b : to diminish in scope or complexity : <u>streamline</u>
   <was urged to *simplify* management procedures>

   c : to make more intelligible : <u>clarify</u>

   — **sim·pli·fi·ca·tion** noun

   — **sim·pli·fi** ·er noun

To simplify: it is all the rage. Take one look online and you
will see books written on simplifying your home, your material
goods, your time, your life, commerce, workflow and your
business. It has become a buzz word in our society that signifies
the desire for things in our life to be prioritized and streamlined,
so that we can get the most out of our lives here on earth. In a

western world where everything can become so fast and blurry, our hearts cry out for the true and simple. We have so much. We may even have acknowledged that God has blessed us, and be grateful, but how do weed out the extra and find out what is truly important? We long for the days when we can slow down and just live...*simply*.

Merriam Webster defines "simplify" as ...to make (something) easier to do or understand...[2] If you picked up this book, then chances are, you have been bombarded with so many thoughts, theories, and methods of evangelism and you are a little (or a lot) confused by the mix of ideas. "How do I really do this thing called evangelism?" you may ask. I believe the answer is simple. It is my goal to prove its simplicity to you throughout this book.

"Another book on Evangelism..." I can almost hear some of you sighing as you are reading this right now. "What haven't I already heard on the subject of personal evangelism?" or better yet, "What could you possibly teach me, seeing as how you are merely a young woman who has only served the Lord for 20 years, and is definitely not a Greek scholar?"

Well, I am so glad that you asked. First of all, let me say that you definitely will not glean anything new from me if you are expecting great theological insight! I hold a two-year certificate from a Bible college, and I have a mere 14 years of ministry experience. Humbly, I can acknowledge that I am still growing and learning daily, and that I have only accomplished a fraction of the Lord's will for my life at this juncture.

---

2   "By permission. From *Merriam-Webster's Collegiate® Dictionary, 11ᵗʰ Edition* ©2015 by Merriam-Webster, Inc. (www.Merriam-Webster.com)."

"You sure are making a phenomenal case against yourself!" you might proclaim. You are right. I am making just such a case, because I truly believe that the only way you will get anything from this book, is if you approach it with an extreme hunger and a desire to see God at work in your life daily through one-on-one evangelism. Any other approach (to inspect my theological doctrine, to gain a fountain of knowledge that you may do nothing with, or otherwise) will result in you only gaining a few small nuggets of truth that may be stored away in the swampy recesses of religious intellect.

I trust that if you have picked up this book, it is for the exact opposite reason. Perhaps you are thinking, "Maybe somehow this book will stir my desire to be a better Christian, disciple, follower of Christ and ultimately better soul winner!"

In my experience, many believers in today's world do not *really* know where to begin in leading someone to the Lord. Over and over, as my husband and I have ministered on the harvest of souls in these end-times, people have asked, "How do you begin to tell someone about God? Do you mean you just start talking to them while in line at the grocery store???" etc. etc. They seem completely unaware as to how to begin the process of witnessing to someone personally, or they have a list of excuses as to why they are not really called to do so. Most of which, as I will explain through the course of this book, are really just that: excuses!

I like how the abstract expressionist painter, Hans Hofman, described the word simplify, "the ability to simplify means to eliminate the unnecessary so that the necessary may speak." So, let's do just that. Let me explain to you what this book is not about, so that we can get down to what it truly is all about.

This book is not set to contradict other methods of evangelism among the church. I am not negating that there are many other powerful moves of God such as servant evangelism, church planting, apologetics, crusades and even church outreach. All have their place, and have ebbed and flowed over the centuries to create powerful tools to bring in the harvest. I believe that many of these are still effective today, as the Spirit leads. These methods are not, and I repeat, ARE NOT what this book is about.

"Simplify Soul Winning" has been put in your hands to strip away every method, religious idea or ideology you or I may have about how we should witness. It is written for the very reason it states: to simplify your outlook on evangelism. This book is written solely to encourage, inspire and equip true Holy Spirit led, one-on-one, daily evangelism. It is the end means that we all, as Christians, should desire. We want true souls won for Jesus…lives truly converted for Him.

For some of you, it is my prayer that this book will kindle a long-term fire for personal evangelism. For others, I hope to reignite or light for the first time a flaming fire within you to passionately share your faith in Jesus everywhere you go. In so doing, I know that you will discover the indescribable joy that there is in sharing your faith as the Spirit of God leads you. If you desire to begin to move in the supernatural river that is called "soul-winning," keep on reading!

"Many good people have become so absorbed in their desire for spiritual depth that they have forgotten that the true ministry of believers is to witness of Christ and to win people to Him."[3]

- T.L. Osborne

3   Osborne, T.L., *Soul Winning*, OSFO Books, 1994, p41

1 | A Simple Prayer

It all began with a simple prayer. "Lord, help me to lead someone to you, personally." My husband and I were pastoring a church in a quaint little beach community. We had been in full-time ministry for over 8 years, and I had begun to see a pattern. We would minister to people in the pulpit, during altar times, next to the hospital bed and on an occasional outreach, but *when* was the last time that I had led someone to the Lord in a one-on-one daily setting? Maybe it was during my days at Bible College? I honestly could not remember. So I prayed this prayer, and it wasn't but a week or so later that I began to see the results.

I was driving into work at the church. My husband ran a business and I ran the daily administrative affairs of our little church. My kiddos were dropped off at school and daycare, and I was eager to get the day started. I remember especially how excited I was to get a jump on the day, because I had a pile of paperwork that needed to be taken care of and I had decided that today was my day to get it done! (Notice I said that *I had decided*. I think this plays a vital component in soul winning: putting our agendas aside. More on this later...)

Before I could go into work, I had to go in for a routine doctor's visit. "Nothing more than fifteen minutes, and I'll be able to get at it!" I thought.

As I pulled into the drive of the doctor's office, I noticed three girls (who looked to be Asian), standing at the entrance of the drive. One of them held their thumb out for a ride to passersby. They were looking at a map, and seemed to be confused and lost. We were in a beach community, so tourists were not that uncommon, but pretty young girls walking or hitchhiking along the highway in a South Alabama town was definitely not a wise move.

I felt prompted by the Spirit of God on the inside of me (I do not mean that I heard an audible voice, but these words rose up out of my spirit), "Go take those girls where they need to go."

"Can I help you girls?" I asked as I rolled down the window.

Sure enough, they were lost. One of the girls spoke English well enough to explain to me that they were here on a foreign exchange job program and had to get to the Social Security offices to get their work visas approved. The closest Social Security office was in a town forty-five minutes away by car, and they were going to try to walk there! I explained that in America that was not a good idea, and that they should probably call a cab. I let them use my phone to call a cab company, and then politely said good-bye and wished them well in their endeavors. I felt good about myself for stopping to help, and went on my way into my appointment.

As I got out of my car to walk into the doctors office, the Spirit of God began to deal with me strongly. "I told you to 'Go take those girls where they need to go.' Why didn't you offer them a ride to the Social Security office?"

All through the doctor's appointment, I reasoned within myself. "Well, I have so much to do today. I had to stop at the them. They happened to live about a mile down the road from the church. The following Sunday they walked to church! Yes, I said, *walked*! Americans don't usually walk anywhere, unless they are in a major metropolitan area. We went on to begin a small Bible study with them. I will say, sadly, that it had to end not too long after as they soon left to go back to their country. These are good, and valid, questions for those in the church. I am not saying that you should ignore them. However I will say that if you are asking them at this juncture, *you missed the point*!

Undoubtedly, the point of this story is: we must stay flexible in our daily schedules to hear the voice of God's Spirit so that we know when there are souls to harvest. We will see these girls again one day in Heaven! The Bible tells us that all the angels in heaven rejoice when one sinner repents (Luke 15:10)! The other, albeit more indirect, point is this: They went back to their predominantly Islamic and closed nation with a message to share and a story to tell that could potentially change tens, hundreds, or even thousands more lives for eternity!

God always asks us to first pray for the harvest, and then to GO into the harvest field. When you make it your prayer to see people come to Jesus, when you hunger and thirst for nothing more than souls won to Him, He is certain to answer that prayer. We see this written in the scriptures plainly. Jesus pleads with His disciples in Matthew 9:37-38 and in Luke 10:2, "Ask the Lord of the harvest, therefore, to send out workers into his harvest field." The first step to reaping harvest is always to pray.

What is amazing is what follows a prayer of this nature. I believe we see a pattern in scripture of praying first, followed by sending. I absolutely love what Matthew 10:1 in The Message goes on to say, "The prayer was no sooner prayed than it was answered. Jesus called twelve of his followers and sent them into the ripe fields." As Christians, we must first begin by praying for the great harvest of souls, and then our eyes are opened to the vast fields around us daily that are already ripe unto harvest! (John 4:35) It is then simply our duty to obey His command to "Go."

So herein lays the challenge of this book: *Will you take the message of Christ's love to a lost and hurting world, as God leads you, today?* If you choose to take this challenge, and make soul winning your heart's cry, I know that God will not disappoint. "Lord, help me to lead someone to the You, *personally,*" is one prayer that God will never refuse.

"You must do it! You cannot hold back. You have enjoyed yourself in Christianity long enough. You have had pleasant feelings, pleasant songs, pleasant meetings, pleasant prospects. There has been much of human happiness, much clapping of hands and shouting of praises - very much of heaven on earth. Now then, go to God and tell Him you are prepared as much as necessary to turn your back upon it all, and that you are willing to spend the rest of your days struggling in the midst of these perishing multitudes, whatever it may cost you."[5]

- William Booth

5   Booth, William (1829 – 1912). *A Vision Of The Lost.* salvationarmy.org.au

2 | Win the Lost, No Matter the Cost

"Why witness?" Any parent will understand the answer to this question... "Because Jesus said to."

I will share a list of scriptural references to give you a foundation of why evangelism should be at the heart of every believer, but I want to focus on this one main point first. We should witness because Jesus told us to witness. It was His last command, His final request. In honor and love of our Savior, we follow His command to, *"Go into all the world"* (Mark 16:15).

Wow! It sounds like such a massive job. Are we really capable? You mean *all* of the world? Yes, but we don't do it alone. We do it collectively, as part of the body of Christ. Each one takes this commission to heart and finds their unique style, receives power from the Holy Spirit and then goes into the part of the world that He has given to them.

Jesus' final words with His disciples, before He ascended into heaven, gave every Christian for all time a purpose during their lifespan: *"GO and make disciples"* (Matthew 28:19, emphasis added).

I remember when I was a young Christian, in my late teens, there was such an incredible zeal to share the gospel with whomever I came in contact. Within a year my entire family heard the plan of salvation. I could not have been content if they didn't hear. Did they all accept it? Sadly, no. However, I was burdened with the thought of not wanting their eternity to be on my hands. An overwhelming desire to share God's love with the world was so evident in me. All who knew me back then could attest to my zeal. I led many to the Lord during those early years.

Here's the incredible thing; I was not perfect (mature) as a Christian! I still smoked cigarettes often. I cursed some. Though I was usually a fairly level-headed person, my temper was less than sanctified. Yet, left and right, I led people to Jesus. Truthfully, I believe that this was because people saw the sincerity and genuineness of my faith despite some of these outward things. I am not advocating that you go out cursing and living an unholy life in order to get people born again. Nonetheless, perhaps there is something to the zeal we have in those early days after coming to know Jesus that we need to harness?

As I began to grow in my walk with the Lord I was able to overcome smoking through self-discipline and the fruit of the spirit. I learned that it wasn't okay to "blow my top" in response to any situation. I grew in my knowledge of the Word and God's will for my life. All of these are very necessary things, and I am so grateful for the discipleship and growth I received as I plugged into church. I began serving in my local church and went to Bible school. However, something happened within me as I reached young adulthood and stepped into ministry. It was gradual, subtle and ever so sneaky, but somehow this thought entered, "I'm doing the work of the ministry… I don't have time to go out soul winning." I knew it was wrong, but I couldn't figure out how to get back into the world, and yet remain separate from it. I was so separated from society, surrounding myself with only Christian and ministry relationships. I barely knew anyone who wasn't born again. How in the world was I to witness to anyone? Was I supposed to embarrass myself and walk up to a *stranger* and just start talking to them?

Yes! I knew that this was true, but how? I struggled with it for years. Though confident in most situations, I did not know how to begin a soul-winning conversation. Do I just blaze in there? Do I try a more 'back door' approach and invite them to an event or Bible study at church?

"That's it!" I decided. I'll just carry invite cards around with me for whatever event the church is holding and invite people as the Spirit of God prompts me. Maybe I'll even plan time to give the cards to people randomly? I was set; this was my new method. It was easy, casual, non-controversial and…it had very *little success*.

I'm just being honest here. Almost no one was taking me up on my invites. Some very sincere-hearted individuals even promised me they would try, but for whatever reason – busy lives, reluctance on Sunday morning, social anxiety – most did not take me up on my offer to come and fellowship with a bunch of believers. Hmm… I wonder why? Even the sound of me saying it now, is incredibly obvious! Most people, no matter how well you doctor up your church to feel like the world, are not fooled into thinking that they want to come and visit your all-Christian club, when they are not yet Christian. Hello!?!

Notwithstanding, I was put back at square one, evaluating my methods of evangelism in full. Maybe, just maybe, I was on to something in those early days of being a Christian?

The Zeal:

I also love what John Wesley had to say about our Christian zeal. "It is no marvel that the devil does not love field preaching! Neither do I; I love a commodious room, a soft cushion, a handsome pulpit. But where is my zeal if I do not trample all these underfoot in order to save one more soul?"

We must come to a point in our lives when we realize that even though God's love is not conditional upon us winning the lost, His heart is for the lost. If His heart is for the lost, then our hearts must be as well.

So true! How many times do we ignore the burning desire (okay, for some, it has become more of a vague simmering thought) to share the love of God that is shed abroad in our hearts with the lost and hurting world right in front of us? Galatians 4:18 expounds on zealousness for us, "It is fine to be zealous, provided the purpose is good."

A few years ago I decided, "Enough is enough." I said within myself, "If I can't cultivate a method of leading someone to Jesus in my own personal life on a regular basis then I am not worthy to minister in the pulpit and ask the same of a congregation." I shared in the introduction how it all began with a simple prayer to lead someone to the Lord. Within a month after that simple prayer I had the opportunity to lead five people personally to Jesus. And the incredible surprise: *it was easy!*

Not one of the encounters was contrived. The second time, I was simply enjoying a coffee with a new girlfriend of mine. She asked some questions about my faith that helped me to locate where she was spiritually. She clearly did not have a personal relationship with God. At that time I was able to share the simplicity of the Gospel. She, like so many, had overcomplicated the Gospel message. When presented with how easy it was to receive God's free gift of salvation, she was ready immediately to pray that prayer! In both of these occurrences, however, as John Wesley so eloquently put it, I had to overcome my soft cushion to go out and win just one more soul!

That zeal within me to win the lost no matter the cost had to be stronger than my fleshly desire for comfort.

Passivity is the great thief of our Christian zeal.

Herein, I believe lays the biggest challenge for most believers in evangelizing: their own fleshly desires and comfort level. We must come to a point in our lives when we realize that even though God's love is not conditional upon us winning the lost, His heart is for the lost. If His heart is for the lost, then our hearts must be as well.

Passivity is the great thief of our Christian zeal. We must stand up inside and say that no matter the feelings of insecurity we may have, we will make a decision to obey his great commission to "Go into all the world."

If my argument does not convince you that you must be witnessing at every possible opportunity, maybe these scriptures will:

Witnessing Scriptures:

- Then the eleven disciples went to Galilee, to the mountain where Jesus had told them to go. When they saw him, they worshiped him; but some doubted. Then Jesus came to them and said, "All authority in heaven and on earth has been given to me. Therefore go and make disciples of all nations, baptizing them in the name of the Father and of the Son and of the Holy Spirit, and teaching them to obey everything I have commanded you. And surely I am with you always, to the very end of the age." (Matthew 28:16-20)

- "As you sent me into the world, I have sent them into the world." (John 17:18)

- We are therefore Christ's ambassadors, as though God were making his appeal through us. We implore you on Christ's behalf: Be reconciled to God. (2 Corinthians 5:20)

- "I am sending you to them to open their eyes and turn them from darkness to light, and from the power of Satan to God, so that they may receive forgiveness of sins and a place among those who are sanctified by faith in me." (Acts 26:17-18)

- "What I tell you in the dark, speak in the daylight; what is whispered in your ear, proclaim from the roofs." (Matthew 10:27)

- "Come, follow me," Jesus said, "and I will send you out to fish for people." (Mark 1:17)

- Then I heard the voice of the Lord saying, "Whom shall I send? And who will go for us?" And I said, "Here am I. Send me!" (Isaiah 6:8)

- "I will follow you, Lord; but first let me go back and say goodbye to my family." Jesus replied, "No one who puts his hand to the plow and looks back is fit for service in the kingdom of God." (Luke 9:61-62)

- As it is written, "How beautiful are the feet of those who bring good news!" (Romans 10:15b)

- Blessed are those who have learned to acclaim you, who walk in the light of your presence, LORD. (Psalm 89:15)

- "No one who has left home or wife or brothers or parents or children for the sake of the kingdom of God will fail to receive many times as much in this age and, in the age to come eternal life." (Luke 18:29b-30)

- Rescue those being led away to death; hold back those staggering toward slaughter. (Proverbs 24:11)

- "You will receive power when the Holy Spirit comes on you; and you will be my witnesses in Jerusalem, and in all Judea and Samaria, and to the ends of the earth." (Acts 1:8)

"He was out of breath pursuing souls."[6]

- A Wesley biographer

6   Krupp, Nate. *You Can Be a Soul Winner Here's How!* Preparing the Way Edition 2004, 1962, p. 174

3 | **Be Bold**

"But you're an extrovert, Ms. Cara." I had more than one sincere church member tell me, when I would encourage them to be a witness. True, I am. I test high as a Choleric and Sanguine on most personality tests. Call me a "lion" and a "golden retriever," if you will, but let me share a little insight into the real "Ms. Cara."

Come back on a quick journey into my childhood with me. Don't worry, we're not going to bring the inner child out to cry or anything, but I want you to see how God can perform a work in someone. I have many memories of a scared and timid little child who ran from her own shadow. When approached by an adult, a new friend, or any number of other situations, my first instinct was to run and hide. This occurred and even became worse into young adulthood.

I can vividly picture it now. The hallways are crowded. I shut my locker door. People are streaming past me as I am headed to my next class as a freshman in high school. I see an acquaintance. Someone I know, but who is exceedingly more "popular" than my awkward little self. I instinctively look down to the ground, hold my books close to my chest and walk by deliberately not making eye contact. Why? I didn't know what to call it then but now I recognize it. I was extremely low in self-esteem. Diagnosis: highly timid with a lack of self-confidence. Cure: a *strong* God dose of God-confidence.

My temperament began to change when I received the Lord. Suddenly, strangers weren't strangers. I could talk to my superior, the unknown person on the bus, or the most popular cheerleader in school. I hadn't any care or concern for what they thought of me, because I knew the One who was with me. The Lord not only believed in me, but he was working within me constantly, and I knew it!

Maybe you experienced it too when you received Jesus and the Baptism of the Holy Spirit? There is something about God coming to live on the inside of you which gives you a confidence in Him like never before. Don't get me wrong; I understand the value of a good personality test or strength identifier in helping you work within an organization or to work with people in general. I also completely understand that you may test strongly as an introvert and that God will use the giftings He has placed in you to serve others. However, when it comes to the ministry of reconciliation, He makes us all extroverts!

We are *all* called to the ministry of reconciliation, and I emphatically believe that means within your sphere of influence, God will give you a "Holy-Ghost boldness" to make you a witness to those around you.

What is boldness? Mirriam-Webster's dictionary defines "bold" as:

: not afraid of danger or difficult situations

: showing or needing confidence or lack of fear

: very confident in a way that may seem rude or foolish[7]

---

7   "By permission. From *Merriam-Webster's Collegiate® Dictionary, 11th Edition* ©2015 by Merriam-Webster, Inc. (www.Merriam-Webster.com)."

Though as Christians, we often think we don't want to seem the latter (rude or foolish), we definitely do need to be able to stand in front of men and women and proclaim our faith with confidence and a complete lack of fear. I believe, if you will allow Him, God will show you what this means for you. For one, it may mean speaking up at work and talking with your coworkers about the difference between relationship and religion. For another, it may mean going door-to-door and praying with people. I knew one person who was convinced that they had a ministry on the golf course.

Personally, I have found that some of my main areas of influence are in the market place (with cashiers, people standing in line or at the coffee shop), while traveling on public transit, or at the Laundromat. For whatever reason, God seems to prompt me most during these times. Speaking to or doing something for another will open the door of conversation to the gospel.

On one occasion, I remember the Holy Spirit prompting me to speak to someone in a Laundromat. It did not seem at the time that I had an open door. So, I did what I have learned to do; I prayed and asked the Lord to open a door of conversation, if that is in fact what He wanted. I waited for the next thirty minutes or so. I continued to fold my laundry and generally went about my business. Just as I was beginning to think they might leave and I would not have the chance, one of their dryers became available. They asked if I wanted to use it, as I was looking to transfer my clothes from the wash. It began a dialogue that seemed relatively natural. We travel, and they could tell I was not from the area. They asked about what we do. I told them we travel with our jobs. I asked about them. Mostly, just chitchat.

From somewhere within me, I heard this, "Ask them about their marriage." I struggled with this for a bit, seeing as how

I am not accustomed to asking complete strangers about their personal lives! I eventually yielded, right as they were packing up their laundry to leave. "Ma'am, do you mind me asking how your marriage is going?" Tears welled up in her eyes.

She spent the next several minutes telling me how she and her husband were going through marital counseling. They had been separated, and were trying to reconcile. It turns out that her husband was a Christian, and had been going to church and praying for her and their marriage. She had grown angry with God over the death of a loved one. Right there in that Mississippi Laundromat, I counseled with her and her husband. I then led her in a prayer of salvation as well as the two of them in a rededication of their marriage to each other with God's help. I encouraged them to go and talk to their pastor that weekend and tell him what had happened and to receive further counsel. It was a wonderful experience. It all began by yielding to the Spirit of God and allowing a boldness from the Holy Spirit to rise up and take control.

I want to take a minute to elaborate on what boldness is not. Being bold is not equal to being rude. Love is not rude (1 Corinthians 13:5). I once knew of a group of Christians that would go around town speaking in tongues loudly and prophesying in public venues. They would often rant and rave throughout a store and get in people's faces telling them that they would burn in hell if they did not repent. Many of the towns' people had labeled this group as a fanatical group and they would not take them seriously. Honestly, most people considered this particular group a joke and a nuisance in the community.

I am a believer in speaking in tongues for encouragement and edification. I believe it is a gift given to the body of Christ, and can also be a sign to the unbeliever when given under the inspiration of the Holy Spirit. This book is not intended to be a study on tongues. Nonetheless, I strongly question this kind of public behavior, as it goes against our commandment to love. As 1 Corinthians 13:1 states, *"Though I speak with the tongues of men and of angels, but have not love, I have become sounding brass or a clanging cymbal."* (NKJV) To the people in those stores, all those "tongues" and "prophesies" were heard as a burdensome noise in their ears.

I know there is a time and place to preach repentance. However, the Law of Love will supersede these kinds of fleshly desires to preach condemnation in such an unbecoming manner. Peace and joy will follow the Law of Love, *and though not everyone will receive*, there will be a clear understanding of your intentions when you share the gospel with a loving and caring attitude. When we speak of boldness, we simply speak of stepping out of our comfort zones and obeying Him to say or do what He instructs us at that moment.

"This is the purpose of the baptism of the Holy Ghost - to empower gospel believers to witness convincingly that Jesus is the Christ, the Son of God, the Savior of the world, risen from the dead and is the author and mediator of redemption."[8]

- T.L. Osborne

8   Osborne, T.L., *Soul Winning,* OSFO Books, 1994, p43

4 | Be Led

Maybe you are one of the many Western-minded individuals who would prefer to "keep your distance" from those you encounter on a daily basis. This is a common mindset in our western culture. We only let those into our lives that we choose to let in. We may even be friendly, cordial and use every-day politeness with strangers, but approaching them about their *religion*? "Won't they feel invaded?" or "Wouldn't that be rude?" you might ask.

Sure, it can be. Approaching someone about his or her religious beliefs can be a very touchy issue. That is why I don't propose that you randomly pass out tracts or walk up to strangers in the grocery store without a specific prompting or leading from the Holy Spirit. Don't get me wrong: you can do this. At times, the Spirit of God may lead you or your group to do this, and you may see some success. But ultimately, when randomly passing out tracts, you are just playing a numbers game in which you are trusting that people's desire to be polite and to accept your tract will lead to the chance that they won't later throw it away when out of sight.

Let me explain *simply* my strategy for evangelism: BE LED.

Yep, you got it. I don't want you to *randomly* do anything. I want you to pray, learn to follow the leading of the Holy Spirit and study the scriptures along the lines of evangelism. Then trust that at the right time, when the Spirit of God prompts you to open the door of conversation, you will have the right words to say to that person.

The Message Bible lays out Luke 9:1-5 this way: *"Jesus now called the Twelve and gave them authority and power to deal with all the demons and cure diseases. He commissioned them to preach the news of God's kingdom and heal the sick. He said, "Don't load yourselves up with equipment. Keep it simple;* **you are the equipment.** *And no luxury inns—get a modest place and be content there until you leave. If you're not welcomed, leave town. Don't make a scene. Shrug your shoulders and move on."* (emphasis added)

He made it really plain to us here. It's as if Jesus were saying, "Listen, you don't have to load yourselves down with years of theological training to go out and preach the gospel! Leave all that heavy doctrine, and those training manuals behind. Keep it simple!! You are all the equipment that you will need!"

Pray, study and then GO as He leads! God is waiting on you.

"Evangelism is summed up in this:
God loving us through his Gospel.
Every message preached should be winged with love."[9]

- Reinhard Bonke

9   Bonnke, Reinhard, *Evangelism By Fire*, E-R Productions LLC, 2008, p138

5 | Be Compassionate

My gaze took me across the Laundromat and I saw a woman folding her laundry. She looked more than a bit frazzled. Her thirty-something years on earth had not been kind to her. While folding laundry for our family of four, and doing my best to hurry to get back to our RV and life traveling on the road, something deep within me welled up. Bringing tears to my eyes, I knew I needed to bless her in some way but was not sure how.

I asked the Lord to show me how and what to say to her, if He wanted me to. Then I went back to folding my laundry and minding my own business. You see, laundry day for me is a day to myself; a day when I'm in my "laundry day" clothes and rarely have any make-up on. A day when the last thing on earth I am thinking about doing is trying to witness.

Time went on and we continued to wash and fold our laundry. Then she stopped me as I passed by to put something in a machine near her. "Excuse me, I noticed you have little boys (she must have seen my piles of little boy clothes too). Would one of them happen to be a size 4? I have this little jacket that doesn't fit my boy any more."

It was a cute little Mickey Mouse jacket that I was just sure my 4 year old would love. I thanked her, and a conversation began.

I asked her if she went to church anywhere in the area. She replied that she didn't have a church. She was new to town and proceeded to tell me her story. She indeed had had a rough life filled with drugs and abuse. She had moved to this little town to start over. I was able to share with Crystal how the best way to "start over" in life was to give her life to God and let Him make something of it.

By the end of our conversation, we had prayed together for her to receive salvation and then she gave me one of the biggest bear hugs I have ever received. She wouldn't let go! She kept thanking me. With tears streaming down her cheeks, she asked me *where she could find a good church*! I was able to get her information and take it to a local pastor to follow up with her.

I believe compassion was the defining moment in that testimony. I stood there in a Laundromat, not desiring to do much but fold my clothes and get back on the road, but I was "moved with compassion" toward this woman. What would have happened if she had handed me that jacket and I just politely thanked her, packed up my clothesbasket and left? Sobering thought.

When I studied the word compassion, I discovered that it is a noun, or a very real and tangible feeling that literally means, "to suffer with." Other definitions include:

…a feeling of *wanting to help* someone who is sick, hungry, in trouble OR sympathetic consciousness of others' distress *together with a desire to alleviate it...* (Merriam Webster, emphasis added) [10]

---

10 "By permission. From *Merriam-Webster's Collegiate® Dictionary, 11th Edition* ©2015 by Merriam-Webster, Inc. (www.Merriam-Webster.com)."

We should learn how to recognize when compassion is rising up within us. This is oftentimes the leading of the Holy Spirit that we are to do something for the person we have compassion towards. This is when compassion (noun) becomes an action (verb). This is when we become God's love in demonstration.

Jesus was moved with compassion often. I encourage you to study these scriptures. He was moved with compassion to bring: healing to the sick (Matthew 14:14), restoration to the hurting and afflicted (Mark 1:41) and provision to the multitudes (Matthew 15:32). In looking at these passages, I saw an underlying motive. Jesus acted on the compassion He had to do a tangible work in people's lives. He then used the opportunity as a doorway to the transformation needed in their lives that only He could bring. Compassion became God's love in demonstration!

Compassion manifests itself in many ways. It is interesting to see that compassion discerns what is really needed; whether that is healing, restoration or provision. At the Gate Beautiful as the beggar sat asking for alms, Peter and John quickly realized that what this man really needed was not money. They saw what the man needed was healing for his body and the changed life that would result! They didn't dismiss this beggar because they didn't have the money to give to him. They didn't ignore him because their purpose in being there was to go to the temple for prayer. Rather, they allowed compassion to well up within them and stopped to give the man what he truly needed. Peter spoke to this man and said, *"Silver and gold I do not have, but what I do have I give you: In the name of Jesus Christ of Nazareth, walk"* (Acts 3:6). Compassion does not simply provide for the natural man's needs, and it does not *always* give the person what he/she is directly asking for, but looks deeper unto the true need and always gives them *Jesus*.

Our family was ministering for a local church in a small rural community. We offered to go door to door and pray for people, inviting families to church as part of an outreach project. After canvassing a wealthy neighborhood with little to no results, we decided to try a set of apartments in a run down area of town. The first people we encountered were a woman in her late forties, her daughter, and young granddaughter. We asked the grandmother, "Is there anything we can pray for you about today?"

She emphatically responded, "Yes! You can pray for the battery in my car. It keeps draining, and I need it to last until payday when I can get a new one."

I looked at her, knowing that her real need was not for a car battery, but to know the One who could provide for that battery and every other need in her life. I said, "Absolutely. We will pray for that." I ministered to her a little bit on the fact that God was an abundant God and could provide for her every need. I then asked, "Before we pray, can I ask you, do you know for sure if you are going to heaven?"

She said she had once received Jesus, but that she was not serving Him now. Her daughter explained that she thought she had lived a good enough life. This is one of the most common misconceptions of the gospel. People think that their self-righteousness will attain entrance into Heaven some day. I told her what Jesus said. *"I am the way and the truth and the life. No one comes to the Father except through me."* (John 14:6) I shared a few more scriptures with her then prayed for the car battery, for the grandmother to rededicate her life to the Lord and for the daughter to receive Jesus for the first time.

They got into the car, and their car started right up! That day, they headed to work with much more than a charged battery. They had a brand new, charged-up, eternal life ahead of them!

Many testimonies of salvation would never have happened if someone didn't stop and allow the compassion of God to move them to action. Allowing compassion to flow will allow God's love to manifest.

A great rule of thumb in all of our witnessing should be the commandment of love. In Mark 12:28-31, we see Jesus approached by a religious scholar of his day. He asked him what the greatest commandment was, to which Jesus said, *"The first of all the commandments is: 'Hear, O Israel, the LORD our God, the LORD is one. And you shall love the LORD your God with all your heart, with all your soul, with all your mind, and with all your strength.' This is the first commandment. And the second, like it, is this: 'You shall love your neighbor as yourself.'* **There is no other commandment greater than these.** *"* (emphasis added)

This is one of the most common misconceptions of the gospel. People think that their self-righteousness will attain entrance into Heaven some day.

I like to say it this way: 1) Love God 2) Love People. If we will follow this basic principle and Jesus' example of love in our every day lives, we will see people who need our help and will make ourselves available to their needs. It will not always be convenient. It may not always seem possible within our natural abilities. We must stop as Peter did and say, *"Silver and gold I do not have, but what I have I give you"* (Acts 3:6). Then, we will see God come through time and again in amazing ways!

"Rejoice in your God-given temperament and use it for God's purposes."[11]

- Rebecca Manley Pippert

11   Pippert, R. M., *Out of the Salt Shaker and Into the World: Evangelism as a Way of Life*, IVP, 1979, p121-22

6 | Be Yourself

I was southbound on Aspen, approaching the 71st street light in Broken Arrow, OK. Turmoil was going on within me. I had only known the Lord a few short years. In that time I had shared God's plan of salvation with most, if not all of my immediate family. Some had accepted salvation. Many had not, and these were the souls that weighed heavily upon my heart and mind day and night. I wanted them to know the love of God as I had experienced it. I wanted to have assurance that I would see them for millennia to come as we shared eternity in Heaven together.

I drove and prayed, burdened with this thought once again. The Spirit of the Lord spoke up within me, "Stop trying to *be* a witness."

"What?" I asked the Lord. In His usual manner, it seemed God spoke to me in riddles. "What do you mean? I thought you said that *we were to be witnesses* in Jerusalem, in Judea, in Samaria and in all the world?"

"I didn't say that." He spoke plainly, "I said...'and you shall be witnesses...' Stop trying to be a witness. I have already made you one."

Suddenly, I saw it. *"But ye shall receive power, after that the Holy Ghost is come upon you: and **ye shall be witnesses** unto me both* *in Jerusalem, and in all Judaea, and in Samaria, and unto the uttermost part of the earth"* (Acts 1:8, KJV, emphasis added). God did not want me to strive to accomplish something that only He could accomplish through me. We can be great witnesses for Him, but first we must allow him to mold and shape us into His image: the person He created us to be. We have to learn to yield to the Holy Spirit, and trust that He will use us in the right time and right place to be a witness. When we do this we *shall be a witness* for Him to the uttermost parts of the earth.

From that day forward, I no longer struggled to say just the right thing and act the right way in order to be a witness to my family. I began trusting that He had already made me a witness when I received Him and was filled with His Holy Spirit. All I had to do was be myself and yield to Him.

So often we want so badly to do the right thing in our Christian walk. God is simply saying to us, "Stop trying and start *being* what I have already made you to be by the power of the Spirit that dwells within you."

I do not believe there is a cookie cutter way to witness. I also don't believe it is scriptural to base Jesus' command for us to "go into all our world" upon our personalities. Wouldn't it be funny if Mark 16:15 read this way: "He said to them, 'If you are particularly outgoing or happen to have a special call or gifting to be bold, then go into all the world and preach the gospel to all creation.'" I am sure that you would agree with me that is not at all what He said. Jesus spoke to all of the followers present and said, "Go into all the world..." This was, simply put, a command for all believers!

I have never been a huge fan of personality tests when it comes to discovering our spiritual giftings. I realize I run a big risk when I say this to the western church, but here is why I believe this: if I looked to my natural personality, I would not be doing what I am today. I would not be writing this book. I would not be a public speaker or preacher! I would never dream of it. When it comes to my natural tendencies, I would rather act like an ostrich and stick my head in the sand than speak in front of others! We can look throughout scripture and see that from Moses the introvert to Paul the choleric; God uses all type of personalities to do His work. Certainly, He is still using every personality type and the combinations in between today.

The key is to be your own unique self in witnessing and to trust God (who is bigger than your personality) to do the work. He truly does take the foolish things of the world to confound the wise (1 Corinthians 1:27). If you will give Him your mouth, He will fill it with wisdom and a boldness to minister it that is beyond you! You will open your mouth to speak and be astonished at how He brings scriptures to your memory. You will begin to witness and see how His boldness rises up within you to share your testimony or to ask someone if you can share how much God loves them. A whole new world of His boldness and His grace to witness will be yours!

I once suffered from severe insecurity in the area of ministering in front of others. I had been in theatre and drama for years. Acting, when I could play the part of a stranger, was one thing – but actually being myself and sharing my story in front of a room full of judgmental people? I despised the idea, and yet knew He was asking me to step out and do this more often.

I was determined to overcome this insecurity. The Holy Spirit chided, "If you will get over yourself, I can use you." Wow! How true it is that so often we esteem the opinions of others too highly. All God asks of us is to not care what others think, and to step out and do what He has called us to do. In the case of every believer, He has called us to preach the gospel to every creature. That job is simple if we can just get over ourselves and let Him move through us.

Oftentimes, the greatest witness is simply to share your story. In most Christian circles we call this our "testimony." We are told by scripture to *"Always be prepared to give an answer to everyone who asks you to give the reason for the hope that you have"* (1 Peter 3:15). A great example of this is the Apostle Paul. We read throughout the book of Acts where Paul, an educated man and an apostle, would not persuade men with his own flattering words, but would share with them his testimony. We see this when he spoke to the crowd in Jerusalem and again to King Agrippa, and throughout the New Testament letters as he shared from his very real and personal struggles of how God helped him to overcome.

> *He has called us to preach the gospel to every creature. That job is simple if we can just get over ourselves and let Him move through us.*

He quantified his heart for approaching others clearly when he said, *"And my speech and my preaching were not with persuasive words of human wisdom, but in demonstration of the Spirit and of power, that your faith should not be in the wisdom of men but in the power of God"* (1 Corinthians 2:4-6, NKJV). Here was Paul, arguably the greatest of apostles, and the man who wrote over one-third of the New Testament, and on numerous occasions he chose to lead with his testimony!

In Galatians 1:23-24 Paul eloquently states the purpose of our testimony: it is used to glorify God. How exciting it is to know that God can take the broken messes of our former life, and use them as powerful witnesses to help change the lives of others! If you haven't already, I challenge you to write down your testimony. Locate the highlights of how God saved you, delivered you and made you new. Then, when the time presents itself, you will be ready to share the power of Christ working in you to bring salvation to the world around you.

"It is the great business of every Christian to save souls. People complain that they do not know how to take hold of this matter. Why, the reason is plain enough; they have never studied it. They have never taken the proper pains to qualify themselves for the work. If you do not make it a matter of study, how you may successfully act in building up the kingdom of Christ, you are acting a very wicked and absurd part as a Christian."[12]

- Charles Grandison Finney

12   Finney, Charles Grandison. *Lectures on Revivals of Religion*, Leavitt, Lord & Co. 1835, p. 159

7 | **Be Prepared**

I can't stress enough how much I don't want you to memorize any one method of evangelism as much as I desire for you to get the principles of evangelism deep into your heart. The method may differ, but the message is always the same: Jesus and Him crucified. There are many great tools out there for learning the plan of salvation. Pick one, and familiarize yourself with it until you would feel confident sharing the plan of salvation with someone. Keep in mind: you may never *feel* ready to begin witnessing. Jesus promised that the Holy Spirit would make you a witnesses (Acts 1:8). Do your part to study and prepare, but when the time comes you will need to be the one to step out boldly, trusting God to fill your mouth with the right words for that individual.

Salvation is a very individual and personal thing. Jesus came to die for each person that has ever existed throughout all time. The plan was the same for each of them; to receive in their heart and confess with their mouth that Jesus is Lord and that God raised Him from the dead. However, the method to reaching each of their hearts will be different. Every person has a deep need that only Christ can fill. You can't find it by yourself. The Spirit of God only can reveal it. As you step out to share the gospel, trust that the One who created the plan will give you the method for the individual before you.

The *Simple* Plan:

His Part...

He Came: We have need of a savior. God made provision for our sin from the beginning of time. His love was not about to let our sin go without a plan of redemption. (John 3:16)

He Died: The Plan was this: Jesus (the Son of God) lived a sinless life for you and I, so that we did not have to. When He died on the cross, He took the infirmities/ weakness of all humankind upon himself. (Romans 6:23)

He Rose Again!: The Provision for our eternal redemption was in the resurrection. Because Jesus rose from the grave, we are able to receive, by faith through grace, that same resurrection power to live this life we have today. (Ephesians 2:8-9)

Your Part...

We Believe & Confess: Our part is simple. We must only believe in our hearts that Jesus is our Lord, and confess with our mouths that God raised Him from the grave. When we do that, we take part in the supernatural transformation called the new birth. We are "born again." We can then rest assured that our eternity will be spent with God in Heaven and that our purpose on earth will be forever transformed. (Romans 10:9-10; John 3:7)

When we present the gospel, this is what we present: God's goodness. We don't argue, condemn or debate. We lay out the simple plan of salvation, and then we ask them to pray with us a *simple* prayer that will start them on their journey with God, and change their eternal destiny.

Below is a list of scriptures that will help you in your witnessing. Memorize and meditate on them. They will be brought back to your memory as you need them in your witnessing (John 14:26). This list is not exhaustive, but a great place to start in learning basic scriptures to help you be a witness!

John 3:16

For God so loved the world that He gave His only begotten Son, that whoever believes in Him should not perish but have everlasting life. (NKJV)

Romans 3:23

for all have sinned and fall short of the glory of God,

I can't stress enough how much I don't want you to memorize any one method of evangelism as much as I desire for you to get the principles of evangelism deep into your heart. The method may differ, but the message is always the same: Jesus and Him crucified.

Romans 6:23

For the wages of sin is death, but the gift of God is eternal life in Christ Jesus our Lord.

Ephesians 2:8-9

For it is by grace you have been saved, through faith—and this is not from yourselves, it is the gift of God— not by works, so that no one can boast.

Revelation 3:20

Behold, I stand at the door and knock. If anyone hears My voice and opens the door, I will come in to him and dine with him, and he with Me. (NKJV)

Romans 10:8-10

But what does it say? "The word is near you, in your mouth and in your heart"...that if you confess with your mouth the Lord Jesus and believe in your heart that God has raised Him from the dead, you will be saved. For with the heart one believes unto righteousness, and with the mouth confession is made unto salvation. (NKJV)

Download your free printable copy of the *Simplify Salvation Tract* @ www.salleyministries.org

"There is nothing that is essential for bringing someone to Christ except the conveying of the knowledge of Christ to them in whatever manner you can. That's why we call witnessing "sharing Jesus Christ." You don't have to have a gospel tract in order to lead a person to Jesus. You don't have to have a Jesus sticker to be a witness. You don't even have to have the Bible in your hand. All you really need is Jesus in your heart. You must keep reminding yourself that it's not the technique or the material that leads a person to Christ. It is the witness of another person who already knows Jesus."[13]

- Arthur Blessit

13 http://www.blessitt.com/E_Books/WitnessingWhereYouAre/Witnessing_Page10. html 17 June 2015.

8 Connect...Locate... Harvest!

Anna was a young employee at Taco Bell™. She was minding the business of her job, fulfilling her duties and straightening the sauce packets. Tracy was a middle-aged English woman on her way home from the shops. She was traversing a long set of stairs with her arms loaded down with shopping bags. Apollos was a Hispanic gentleman traveling the airlines on his way home from visiting family in Mexico. What did these three have in common? They all were about to have a divine encounter to receive Jesus on a real and personal level.

When we teach the process of soul winning, we break it down into three simple steps. Connect...Locate...Harvest! The first step is to connect with the person God is leading you to minister to. DO NOT SKIP THIS STEP. It is vital. There are many methods of evangelism, and all have merit, but for your method to have a greater measure of impact I believe that connection is a crucial step. You have to first find a point of interest, source of conversation, or means of connecting with the person on a real and personal level. This doesn't have to be a deep connection. Some people seem fine to begin conversations about their dogs or favorite football team, while others will require a deeper connection. In these cases, God may lead you with a word of knowledge, or give you special insight into a need that you can then ask to pray for them.

For some, this is an easy process. They are naturally sanguine, and jumping into conversation with a complete stranger is a breeze. For others, this may take some cultivating. I recommend starting with some easy warm ups. Begin by looking for conversation starters in the grocery line or sitting next to someone at a bus stop. Some of you might be in a panic at this point. "What do I say to them?"

You might start by saying, "It sure is cold out today, isn't it?" or "That is such a cute little puppy!" to the person walking a dog in the park. These little conversation starters can open wide the doors to present the gospel. "Well, what if they don't stop to chat?" you may ask. Simple: then they are NOT the person that God is leading you to minister to at that moment. Smile. Say, "have a great day," and move along.

Let me ask you this: What if it does lead to something more? What if they begin chatting about their love for animals, or how they wish it could be warm and sunny again? Then, you have created a moment in which you can begin looking for an opportunity to share the love of Christ with them.

The next step is to locate. This may start with one of the questions we have mentioned previously, such as, "Has anyone ever told you how much God loves you?" When they respond, you are able to quickly identify where they are in their spiritual journey. For instance, to the man that replies, "I don't think God could ever love someone like me," you now know that this is a man that is in need of meeting a loving God that loves even the most unlovely or unlikely of people.

If a young woman responds with, "Yes, my momma has told me," as Anna at Taco Bell™ shared with Brian one day, you know that she has more than likely heard of a God that loves.

Your next question is to ask whether she has received this God as her own Savior. In this case, Brian asked Anna "Is your momma a Christian?" When Anna said, "Yes," Brian said, "Well, are you?" She quickly replied "Not yet." He said, "Well, do you want to be?"

Locating someone spiritually so that you can give them instructions on how to make Heaven is a lot like finding out where someone is coming from before you give them directions to your house. If they are coming from the north end of town, you will give them entirely different directions than if you they are coming from the south. This is why we must locate a person before sharing the gospel message with them.

Lastly, we harvest! This is our goal. This is our motive: more souls in to the kingdom of God, more people coming to know Him! Harvest time is outlined in the previous chapter, Be Prepared. Here, we are taking whatever

Locating someone spiritually so that you can give them instructions on how to make Heaven is a lot like finding out where someone is coming from before you give them directions to your house.

method or strategy we are comfortable with, and as the Holy Spirit leads, we share the Good News of Jesus with the person we are encountering. Harvest time is the exciting part, but we must not skip the first two steps of connecting and locating to get here.

I will let you know that Anna prayed to receive Jesus while "on the clock" at work. Brian asked if she wanted to be a Christian as her mom was. She said, "Now? I'm at work!" He said, "All the better. You'll get paid to get born again!" She bowed her head right next to the sauce packets and prayed the sinner's prayer.

When I approached Tracy, I exclaimed, "These steps sure will get you winded, won't they?" I asked my boys to help her with her shopping bags. After noticing that the boys were so "well mannered" I was able to let her know that we were in the United Kingdom to tell people about Jesus. She said she would like to receive this Jesus and prayed with me right there on the stairs in front of her neighborhood.

Apollos and I had a lovely conversation about his family and life. He had led a long life of empty religion. He knew he needed God, and though I not once mentioned his sin or tried to condemn him, He kept saying, "I need to repent don't I?" The Holy Spirit had been working on his heart, drawing him to Himself for some time. Apollos was ripe for harvest! Our conversation on the plane led to him praying a prayer to receive the Lord for the first time, just shortly before we landed.

"If the testimony of Christ is only shared within the walls of the sanctuary, then the majority of unconverted people will never discover Christ in their lives because they will not be present (at your church)."[14]

- T.L. Osborne, Soul Winning

14   Osborne, T.L., *Soul Winning*, OSFO Books, 1994, p.61

9 | Taking it to the Streets

Two separate pastors approached my husband nearly simultaneously. One was located in the United Kingdom and the other in Texas. "Would you come and conduct a soul winning training for our church?" Of course! We willingly obliged. The dates were set, and the travel arrangements were made. How exciting it was to have the opportunity to impart these strategies we had learned with our own family into the lives of others!

I love to see how God works on your heart to create and bring about His plan. Earlier that year, I had begun scripting this book and formulating a plan for an accompanying workbook by His leading. We had no seminars on the calendar, but knew that God was going to use these materials in some sort or fashion. The materials were nearly ready for the seminars, as a result of taking this step of obedience, even before these pastors called.

After assimilating the first draft of the workbook Brian took off to the United Kingdom for that first workshop by himself. He preached a Friday night session. No sweat for him, as preaching and teaching is what he excels at and what God has graced him to do. He taught the Saturday morning session with great anticipation, as the plan was to take teams, two-by-two, out on the streets directly following the classes.

Pause…Deep breath…Here goes!

He confesses how nervous he was, and quite frankly, I was glad he was the one leading it and not myself! We had taken our little family of four out on the streets and led one after another to the Lord, proving that this witnessing thing works. We knew that we wanted to do this very thing; training others to put these simple strategies into practice. Now it was time to "either put up or shut up" as the saying goes.

Brian passed out five tracts to each team with the *Simple Plan* of Salvation on them. He then gave the instructions for them to follow the principles outlined in this book: BE LED, BE BOLD, BE YOURSELF, BE COMPASSIONATE, AND BE PREPARED. He said to them, "Don't worry about passing out every tract. These are just tools. If you come back with every tract, but you were able to lead someone to Jesus, we will be thrilled!" They were to go out into the streets for exactly 30 minutes then reconvene at the church auditorium to share their testimonies, no matter the results.

At the end of thirty minutes, Brian testifies, he was discouraged. He had taken a young man who was very zealous with him. Though he did have a divine appointment with a Catholic priest that was ministering in an area he was later going to, he came back without a story to share of leading someone to Jesus. However, the rest of the teams had quite a different experience. Each one made their way back and each and *every one of them* had a testimony of sharing God's love with someone and seeing them receive Jesus! For many of these teams this was his or her first time ever to see someone born again personally!

He called me later that day to give me the update. I will never forget that conversation. I was standing in the kitchen of the little missions house we were staying in. As tears streamed down my face, he relayed one by one the testimonies of these courageous teams of soul winners.

In this chapter, I have included a few short testimonies from some of our seminars since then. It amazes and humbles us every time we hear a new testimony and see how God is using this message to inspire and equip the church to bring in the harvest. Time and again, we hear these words, "It's so *easy!*" or "It really *works!*" People overcome their fears of speaking to others, and relational walls tumble as they begin connecting with the world around them. Then they begin sharing the good news of the gospel with ease and simplicity.

One young lady was walking through a park near their church in Bedford, England for the session out on the streets. She felt led to go and sit on a park bench. There she spoke to a Muslim man and began talking about the weather. After a minute of discussing the chilly spring air, she asked him if anyone had ever told him about the love of God. This man had been told by several of his friends about Jesus, and that God loved him, but said that he was not ready yet to receive Him. She felt led to ask him about his family. This grown man began crying, as he shared how his wife and child had recently died. After a few minutes of sharing his story, He said "I believe that God led you to me," and then expressed that He was ready to receive Jesus. The young girl who led this Muslim man to the Lord expressed how incredible it was to go out in the power of the Holy Spirit and see how He had prepared the way for her to share the gospel. She also stated that, "Normally, I wouldn't have put myself in that situation, but taking yourself out of your normal comfort zone can have such an impact on someone else's life."

One woman, who was a teacher by profession, was led to witness to a teenage student she saw on the streets. She called this student a "terror" in the classroom. She testified that the Lord told her to "take her teacher hat off" and "put her friend hat on." She approached the student and shared this with her. The student wept as the teacher shared the love of God with her, and then she was able to lead her to Jesus!

Another couple out on the streets ran into a gentleman who was very new to town. He was already a Christian, but did not have a church home yet. The couple asked if he would like for them to pick him up for church the next morning. He was thrilled at the prospect, and they added him to their carpool and to their church the following Sunday!

Another student felt led to go pray with her 93-year-old grandmother after the personal evangelism course. She said she went in and she prayed a sinner's prayer with her. Her grandmother said, "Wow! Now I am back right with Him." I guess she had walked with God as a young girl, but had not lived her life for him. She will spend eternity with her Creator now! It...is...never...too...late.

Ethan, a student at Bible College, shared with me after taking the *Simplify Soul Winning* course: "I led someone to the Lord on the way to church. I felt prompted to go talk to this man. I asked him about his dog, and we began to talk. After a minute, I was able to lead him in a sinner's prayer. I just want you to know, IT WORKS!"

Ava, a young and bright 6-year-old girl, came up to me on the McDonald's™ playground. We had completed a short lesson on Simplify Soul Winning with the children for the seminar but during the break had taken the kids to play and have lunch. It was time to go and we were rounding the children up to head back to the church. Ava looked up at me with big sincere eyes, while tugging on my shirt. "Mrs. Cara, but I haven't told anyone about Jesus!"

"Normally, I wouldn't have put myself in that situation, but taking yourself out of your normal comfort zone can have such an impact on someone else's life."

Her pure heart gripped me. I thought, "I can't disappoint her!" So I told her to follow me as I scanned the room for someone we could talk to. I saw a Hispanic gentleman standing in the corner. We boldly walked up to him. Ava shared that Jesus loved him, then I spoke with him for a minute and he prayed to receive Jesus. This story still melts my heart at the thought of Ava's child-like faith. Oh, that we would all catch her zeal to tell people about Jesus!

I hope that these stories encourage you, as they did myself, that following God's simple strategy for soul winning is effective and easy for any and all who will put it into practice. Since then, countless others have gone on to testify of the ease with which they were able to share their faith after hearing the *Simplify Soul Winning* message.

"The great thing, if one can, is to stop regarding all the unpleasant things as interruptions of one's 'own,' or 'real' life. The truth is of course that what one calls the interruptions are precisely one's real life -- the life God is sending one day by day."[15]

- C.S. Lewis

15   Lewis, C.S. *The Collected Works of C.S. Lewis,* Thomas Nelson, 2004

10 | Life Interrupted

I began to see a pattern with my witnessing. It happened most frequently when I was feeling tired and like I had nothing personally to give. For instance, He would lead me to reach out in the Laundromat with my laundry day clothes and no makeup, on my way to a busy work day, or while sitting next to someone in the airport when all I wanted to do was read my book and rest. "Lord, why do you always ask me to step out and witness to someone when I least feel like it?" I asked one day. His response came to me clearly, and has been made clear as I studied the scriptures: *"because there is a Biblical principle at play."* I was reminded of the scripture in Proverbs 11:25 *"Whoever brings blessing will be enriched, and **one who waters will himself be watered.**"* (ESV, emphasis added) Suddenly, I saw it! Time and again, I have watched as I ministered salvation to someone at what seems like one of my lowest or weakest points. In that moment, I receive a fresh infusion of the Spirit that sends me on my spiritual walk with renewed vigor! In that moment of watering another soul, I myself am watered.

Jesus taught and illustrated this same principle with the woman at the well. Jesus had stopped at a well in Sychar. Sychar was a Samaritan village, a seemingly nowhere place on His journey from Judea to Galilee. In the natural, it was just a stop on their route from point A to point B. However God had a different plan, and a divine encounter was awaiting Jesus and his disciples. God wanted to interrupt their life for a couple of days, and the result was a citywide revival!

> *In that moment, I receive a fresh infusion of the Spirit that sends me on my spiritual walk with renewed vigor! In that moment of watering another soul, I myself am watered.*

Jesus was hungry, so he sent his disciples after some food. (Here's a side thought that my husband likes to point out: they must have been some really bright disciples, because Jesus sent all twelve of them just to go find lunch!) Jesus had been walking all day. He was probably tired and thirsty, as well. The Samaritan woman approached the well. I believe, at this point, Jesus was simply acting out of his natural need for hydration. He said, "woman would you give me a glass of water?" She is astounded that He, being a Jew, would cross His cultural and religious boundaries to speak to her, a Samaritan. He replies to her that He has "living water." So here we first see Jesus reference a spiritual well that will quench a thirst like nothing else can.

This is just the beginning of a dialogue that turns this normal, everyday encounter into a supernatural, life changing experience for this woman. I encourage you to read the story in John 4 in its entirety. You will find it is a very captivating example of Jesus being led by the Holy Spirit through a word of knowledge in personal evangelism.

When the disciples return, they ask Jesus if he wants to eat. To which He replies, "I have food of which you do not know." They look at each other dumbfounded (I imagine) and say, "What? Did you already eat!?" This is my paraphrase, of course, but I hope you are getting the picture. Jesus was already refreshed! He had stopped to listen to the Holy Spirit in ministering life to this woman. As a result, the Spirit of God strengthened Him supernaturally, giving Him water for his soul and food for his flesh in order for him to go on doing the work He was doing.

I have watched this happen countless times in my own soul winning experiences. I will leave the house depleted. Wondering how I am going to get the strength to do all that lies in front of me, but when I obey the Holy Spirit and step out in faith to witness to someone, I come away with a renewed strength to tackle the rest of my agenda. Better yet, sometimes my agenda no longer even matters! I have watered the well of another, and I am watered in return.

I want to leave you with one final thought, as I close this book: LIFE INTERRUPTED.

Do you remember the Kyrgystan girls I spoke of in the beginning of this book? You know, the ones who so *rudely* disturbed my busy day! (I am being sarcastic, of course.) Well, I would like to revisit that account for just a bit. Do you remember how busy I was, and the mound of paperwork that awaited me at work? Do you remember the doctor appointment and the coffee that I stopped to get? I had an agenda, and although it seemed to be a good one, it was not God's plan for that day. God's plan was for me to encounter three young women in need of a Savior. God's plan was for me to help them on their journey *toward Him*. Quite simply: the salvation moment that came that day for those three beautiful girls, would not have happened if I hadn't let my life be interrupted. Frankly, most of the encounters I have had in sharing the love of God with individuals over the years would not have occurred had I not stopped to listen and obey His leading. How many souls are present in the streets and market places of your community waiting on you to live your *life interrupted*?

"Life Interrupted"

I woke up early this morning
  Glad to tackle the day.
My lists and task awaited
  Pressing, they seemed to say,
"Come! Now! I must be done!
  No time you have to waste."
So I gathered, cleaned and planned.
  Task's voice heeded, I made haste.
I hurried about *my* business,
  But something seemed amiss.
Was I forgetting something?
  Did I omit an item from my list?
And then I leaned in to it:
  That familiar gentle voice,
"There's a detour up ahead.
  It's not yours, but is *My* choice.
A life hangs in the balance.
  Eternal destiny is at stake.
Will you please take time to follow,
  Or will your list you take?
I stopped there in my footsteps.
  Adjusted my compass, it seemed.
Direction righted, I followed.
  An eternal destiny was gleaned!
Now, dear reader, please ponder:
  Will you be guided by *His* choice?
Will you let your life be
  Interrupted by *His* voice?

Bibliography

Unless otherwise stated, Scripture quotations are taken from the Holy Bible, New International Version®, NIV® Copyright ©1973, 1978, 1984, 2011 by Biblica, Inc.® Used by permission. All rights reserved worldwide.

Scripture quotations marked "MSG" or "The Message" are taken from The Message. Copyright 1993, 1994, 1995, 1996, 2000, 2001, 2002. Used by permission of NavPress Publishing Group.

Scripture taken from the New King James Version®. Copyright © 1982 by Thomas Nelson. Used by permission. All rights reserved.

Scripture quotations marked (ESV) are from The Holy Bible, English Standard Version® (ESV®), copyright © 2001 by Crossway, a publishing ministry of Good News Publishers. Used by permission. All rights reserved.

Bonnke, Reinhard, *Evangelism By Fire*, E-R Productions LLC, 2008

Booth, William (1829 – 1912). *A Vision Of The Lost.* salvationarmy.org.au

Earley, Dave, and Rod Dempsey. *Disciple Making Is--: How to Live the Great Commission with Passion and Confidence.* B & H Publishing Group, 2013, p. 135

Finney, Charles Grandison. *Lectures on Revivals of Religion,* Leavitt, Lord & Co. 1835, p. 159

Kennedy, D James Ph. D., *Evangelism Explosion*, Tyndale House Publishers, Inc. 1970, 1977, 1983, 1996

Krupp, Nate. *You Can Be a Soul Winner Here's How!* Preparing the Way Edition 2004, 1962, p. 174

Merriam-Webster's Collegiate® Dictionary, 11th Edition ©2015 by Merriam-Webster, Inc. (www.Merriam-Webster.com)."

Osborne, T.L., *Soul Winning*. OSFO Books, 1994

Pippert, R. M., *Out of the Salt Shaker and Into the World: Evangelism as a Way of Life*, IVP, 1979

Telford, John. "Wesley Center Online." *The Life of John Wesley.* N.p., n.d. Web. 23 June 2015.

http://www.blessitt.com/E_Books/WitnessingWhereYouAre/Witnessing_Page10.html 17 June 2015

CPSIA information can be obtained
at www.ICGtesting.com
Printed in the USA
FSOW04n1840191016
26345FS